# Cragside

*Northumberland*

THE NATIONAL TRUST

# 'The Palace of a Modern Magician'

Cragside was the home of an extraordinary man – William George Armstrong (1810–1900). He was a scientist and technical innovator of genius, one of the most successful industrialists of his generation, and the principal founder of Newcastle's Victorian wealth and of its advances in education and health provision. Yet Lord Armstrong seems to have been unaffected by his success. Those who knew him remarked on his friendly, businesslike approach, his good nature, and his devotion to science. If he had been more eccentric or flamboyant or disagreeable, then he would be better remembered as one of the greatest Victorians.

## A passionate gardener

Armstrong's wife, Margaret Ramshaw, was the daughter of a Bishop Auckland engineer. A devoted couple, their marriage was to last almost 50 years, and together they created two

*Margaret Ramshaw, who married William Armstrong in 1835 and helped to lay out the gardens at Jesmond Dene and Cragside; by H. H. Emmerson*

*William Armstrong in old age; painted by Mary Lemon Waller in 1898*

extraordinary homes: the first at Jesmond Dene on the edge of Newcastle, and then at Cragside. Perhaps because they had no children, we know too little about Lady Armstrong. Clearly, she played an important anchor role, supporting her husband in his hectic life. Generally liked and respected, and far from being just a retiring wife, she was a highly capable household manager and hostess. She was also an enthusiastic and knowledgeable gardener. It seems to have been her passion for plants, as much as her husband's vision, which was crucial to the creation of their gardens. It was with Lady Armstrong that garden

## Where modern living began

The house at Cragside combines outstanding architectural design, pioneering furnishings and fittings, and the most advanced technical devices of the day. Here water power was first used to provide electricity in 1878 – the first 'hydro-electricity'. Armstrong was a friend of Sir Joseph Swan, who fitted Cragside with his new filament light bulbs. Visitors would gape, yet most of the technical wonders had a simple purpose – to limit routine tasks, lighten loads, and improve efficiency. Servants had lifts to get coal to bedrooms, electric gongs to announce meals, automatic turnspits, even an internal telephone system. They tended to stay.

Water is the theme that links Armstrong's recreations with his business endeavours, and the foundation of his industrial success. Here at Cragside, combining landscape improve-ments with experimental technology, Armstrong first united elements which were to become the norm for good houses in the following century: hot and cold running water, central heating, mechanical aids and electricity. No wonder one commentator called Cragside 'the Palace of a Modern Magician'. For it was here that modern living began.

*(Right) Armstrong in the Library at Cragside, which was lit by electricity from 1880*

suppliers corresponded, and she had most opportunity to direct the garden works at Cragside. She helped to transform bare hillsides and narrow denes into one of the finest gardens of Victorian England.

## For all to enjoy

In 1977 the house, with 911 acres of land around it, and two farms in the Coquet valley, passed to the Treasury in part-settlement of death-duties. It was then transferred to the National Trust through the auspices of the National Land Fund, aided by a generous gift from the 3rd Lord Armstrong. Substantial help was received from the Historic Buildings Council during the long restoration that followed. The house was first opened to the public in 1979. In 1991 the formal terraced gardens, glasshouses, the original estate manager's house, and parkland were acquired and reunited with the rest of the estate.

# Armstrong the man

## *Industrialist and innovator*

### Origins

Armstrong's life completed a classic story of a family's search for success and then respectability and position. His father, also named William Armstrong, was the son of a tenant farmer at Wreay near Carlisle, who had started work as a clerk with a firm of corn merchants on Newcastle's quayside and, through hard work and enterprise, had risen to own the business. His sensible choice of wife was Anne Potter, the daughter of a colliery owner. Equally important was his broad circle of friends in a generation which contributed both to the mercantile and industrial growth of Newcastle and also to the broadening of its intellectual life. Entering local politics in 1835, he took a particular interest in the management of the Tyne, to which Newcastle's prosperity was so closely linked, and his endeavours were recognised when he became mayor in 1850.

### From lawyer to engineer

Their second child and only son, William George, was born in 1810 at 9, Pleasant Row, Shieldfield, then on the edge of Newcastle. As the boy grew, so did his father's ambition that he should advance socially away from 'trade' to a professional career. He wanted his son to follow the law and arranged for him to join the firm of his closest friend, Armorer Donkin, a prosperous

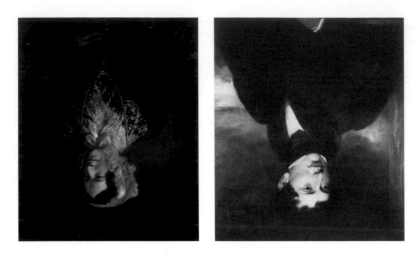

*(Right) William Armstrong, painted by James Ramsay in 1831, when he was still a law student*

*(Far right) Armstrong's mother, Anne Potter, who was the daughter of a colliery owner*

Newcastle solicitor. William George completed his legal training in London under his brother-in-law, William Henry Watson, before returning to Newcastle in 1833 to join Donkin's partnership.

Donkin found Armstrong a capable and efficient lawyer, but was wise and kind enough to realise where the young man's real interests lay, and to allow him scope to develop his enthusiasm for science and mechanics. Through his observations and experiments in identifying what later became known as the Armstrong Effect, Armstrong was elected a Fellow of the Royal Society at the age of 36 and while still practising as a solicitor. Gradually, through involvement with companies dealing with water supply and cranes, the lawyer became an engineer.

### A practical scientist

In order to move into manufacturing, in 1847 he bought land at Elswick by the Tyne, and the partnership W. G. Armstrong & Company was established. Armstrong had a rare combination of talents: his fascination with scientific enquiry was linked to a clear understanding that science should be directed to practical purposes; he had the flexibility of mind to see how to use existing technologies in new ways; he could see what people needed and he recognised mass-production opportunities; his technical authority and personal magnetism convinced investors; he showed shrewd judgement in selecting staff; and, above all, he had the energy, drive and vision to set up and lead a successful company.

If occasionally he showed great intransigence in negotiation with his workforce (as in provoking the engineers' strikes of 1871 in favour of a nine-hour day), this probably resulted from frustration with impeded progress. He may also have resented what he would have regarded as ingratitude; but the early Victorian paternalism in industrial relations in which he believed — he had built an institute and schools at Elswick — was becoming out of date. Certainly he learned from such mistakes. As he matured and prospered, he showed a natural generosity of spirit in disposing of his wealth to include the development of benefits for his workers and their dependants — and indeed to the whole Tyneside community. He came to be liked and respected by all who knew him personally.

*(Above) Armstrong's Elswick works on the Tyne, which was the heart of his business empire, by T. M. Hemy, c.1880*

*(Below) Armstrong's 'hydro-electric' machine was designed to generate static electricity. It began his lifelong interest in electricity*

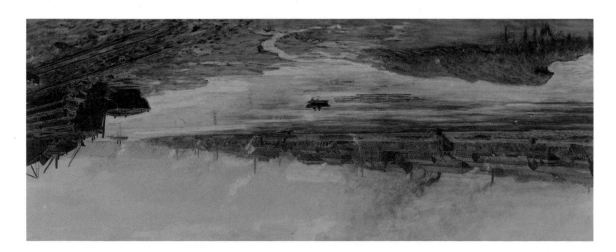

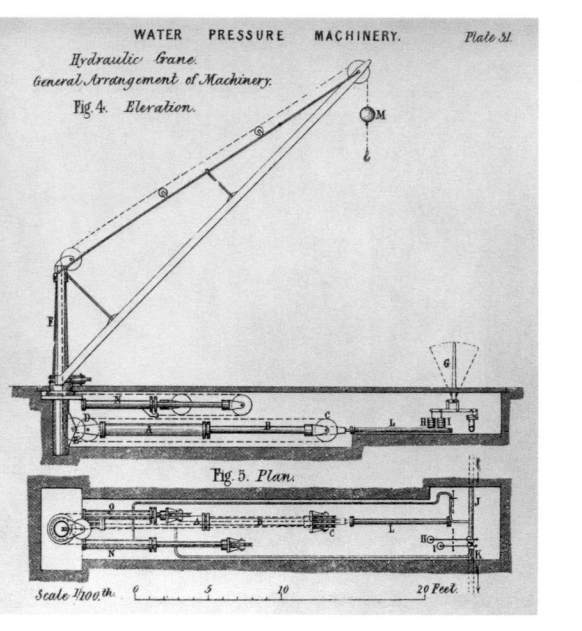

WATER PRESSURE MACHINERY. Plate 31.

Hydraulic Crane.
General Arrangement of Machinery.
Fig. 4. Elevation.

Fig. 5. Plan.

Scale 1/100th. 0 5 10 20 Feet.

*Armstrong's hydraulic crane, which was first used in the Newcastle docks in 1846*

## Harnessing the power of water

Armstrong's first success was in applying hydraulics to lifting heavy weights. Perhaps his greatest achievement and, in the words of his biographer, Peter McKenzie, 'the key to the general adoption of hydraulic systems', came in 1850–1, when he introduced a hydraulic accumulator, a means of increasing water pressure (and thus power). This made it unnecessary either to have a natural high head of water or to build a tower. Success with dockside cranes led to larger projects involving the moving of objects so large that many believed them unmovable: dry-dock gates, and moving bridges such as Newcastle's Swing Bridge (1876) and London's Tower Bridge (1894).

## The great gun-maker

Armstrong's next achievement was in gun-making and, more specifically, in the application of small-arms technology – rifled barrels and breech-loading – to larger guns. He produced his first prototype, the Number One Gun, in 1855. Within three years his guns were achieving barely credible results. Although half the weight of conventional guns, and therefore much more manoeuvrable, they could project a shell of equal size three times the distance, using only half the charge; and they were much more accurate. The type was adopted by the army; Armstrong was appointed Chief Engineer of Rifled Ordnance and knighted in 1859. Ten years later, after a number of accidents caused by incorrect closing of the breech, conservative elements in the army forced a return to muzzle-loading. Armstrong resigned his appointment, released his patents to the government, and concentrated on technical advances and private industrial progress. When, after a further ten years, the army returned to breech-loading, Armstrong was already making some of the largest guns in the world – for overseas customers.

## Warships for the world

Armstrong's final industrial achievement was in building warships. Starting in partnership with the firm of Charles Mitchell of Walker in 1868, he steadily expanded this aspect of his work. Although Armstrong gradually withdrew in favour of his able assistant and successor, Sir Andrew Noble, it was his hydraulic expertise which was developed to ease the operation of ever larger guns. Steel-making was added to the capabilities. The two firms came together in 1882, and the last fifteen years of the century saw the highpoint of the united firm's formidable international reputation. Its only serious rival was Krupps of Essen, a firm directly subsidised by the German government. Armstrong's achievements were recognised with a peerage in 1887.

By the end of the 19th century the firm employed 25,000 workers, occupied 300 acres of land, and was building the largest and most powerful battleships of their time for customers all around the world. Long shadows were cast forward: half the Japanese ironclads in the victorious naval war against Russia in 1905 were built by Armstrongs, and a few were still in commission at the time of the attack on Pearl Harbor.

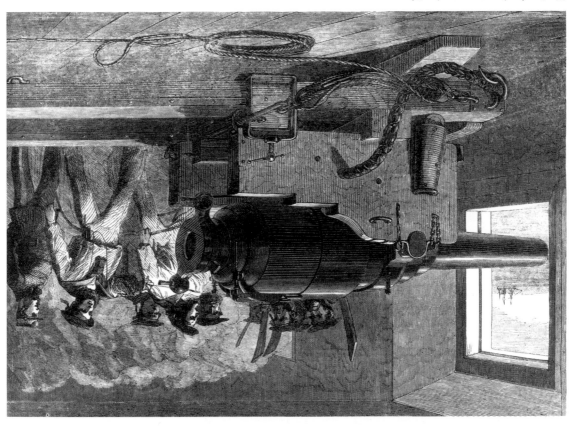

Testing the Armstrong gun in 1862

Armstrong supplied the machinery to raise London's Tower Bridge; by W. L. Wyllie, 1894

# Creating Cragside

Armstrong achieved great wealth and spent his money like many successful men of his day, on his family, on his homes and on his collections. Until the 1870s his main home was at Jesmond, then on the edge of Newcastle. There he and Lady Armstrong created a comfortable home with splendid gardens (eventually to be given in two parts to the city of Newcastle and now known as Armstrong Park and Jesmond Dene). He also built a banqueting house overlooking the Dene to entertain larger numbers of guests (which suggests that the house, which has now completely disappeared, was not very large).

Cragside at first was intended as just a holiday home. In 1863 Armstrong, having had no proper holiday for fifteen years because of the demands of his business, decided to take an angling trip to Rothbury. His sickly boyhood had been marred by a bad chest. 'More than once,' he remembered, 'an apparently incurable cough was quickly removed by coming to Rothbury, and had it not been for its curative

*(Right)  A romantic watercolour of Cragside from the Debdon Burn. It was the river that first drew Armstrong to Rothbury*

> 'I believe I first came here [to Rothbury] as a baby in arms, and my first recollections consist of paddling in the Coquet, gathering pebbles on its gravel beds, and climbing among the rocks on the Crag.'
>
> Lord Armstrong, 1888

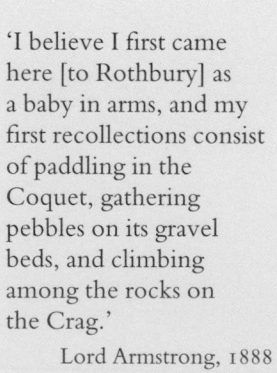

effect there would have been no Cragside'. The trip revived happy memories of annual family visits to Armorer Donkin, and of angling and exploring along the river. On impulse he decided to buy a few acres in the Debdon valley and to build a small house which he might use for angling holidays.

As the potential of the house and its setting grasped Armstrong's imagination, and as railway transport made journeys to Newcastle easy, so Cragside grew. It became the focus for the Armstrongs' building and planting activity, and soon, too, their principal residence. Nor was it just a large house with a huge ornamental garden, for, as Armstrong's purchases of land progressed, so Cragside became the centre of a

large estate with property in Rothbury and more than twenty farms in Upper Coquetdale.

Armstrong's main personal expenditure was at his homes, and because he and his wife had no family of their own, they became very close to the family of his sister. She had married a distinguished London lawyer, William Henry Watson, but she died quite young. Eventually it was her grandson, William Watson, who added Armstrong to his name, and succeeded Lord Armstrong at Cragside. His great-uncle's title died with him, but, for outstanding benefactions and public service, he was himself ennobled in 1903 as the 1st Baron Armstrong of Bamburgh and Cragside. He was succeeded by his son and grandson, on whose death in 1987 the title became defunct.

## Armstrong the collector

Cragside grew to accommodate Armstrong's famous collection of contemporary British art. Armstrong was an enthusiastic collector. He did not rely wholly on agents to acquire pictures, but, when possible, would attend an auction himself. A surviving letter, written to his wife on 23 April 1875, shows how exciting he found such occasions:

The first day's sale of the Manley Hall collection has come off today. I only bid for one picture & got it. It is a landscape by Müller not large but very fine. Price 600 g[uinea]s. I reserve my strength for tomorrow when the most important pictures will be sold. I fear there will be severe competition for Millais's Jephthah which is exciting great admiration. It is so fine that I must have it even at the £4000 which Emmerson said I would give. But whatever I give I wish to keep as secret as I can.

He was successful in acquiring both *Jephthah's Daughter* (for 3,800 guineas) and another

*Jephthah's Daughter by Sir John Everett Millais was one of Armstrong's most expensive purchases*

painting by Millais, *Chill October*. These two pictures eventually became central to the display in the Drawing Room at Cragside alongside works by many of the best-known artists of the day, including Edwin Landseer, Peter Graham, Henry Nelson O'Neil and Lord Leighton.

### Armstrong the angler

'... selected Rothbury for various reasons, the beauty of the scenery, the healthiness of the place, his early childhood's associations (for he was brought there as a boy by his parents, and the memory of many a happy day's trout fishing with his father on the banks of the silvery winding Coquet). Fishing was always the sport for him, and he even confessed to having had some days of poaching in forbidden waters. To the end of his days it retained its fascination for him, and I went out fishing with him one day when he was considerably over eighty.'

Winny, Lady Armstrong, 1906

# Life at Cragside

The house was so advanced for its time and became so well-known that it was described in the publications of the day. Its fame was such that the Armstrongs were accorded the extra-ordinary honour (especially for someone not yet a Lord) of hosting the Prince and Princess of Wales and their five children for three days in August 1884. That occasion, though unusual in the scale of the visit and the prominence of the guests, gives some idea of why Cragside was such a remarkable place to stay.

Apart from the Drawing Room, completed just in time for the royal visit, the rooms at Cragside are not large. The house is not intended for formal processions or display. Visits took the form of relaxed country weekends with sporting pursuits for the men and walks in the pleasure grounds for the ladies. There was boating on the lakes, which were stocked with trout for angling. There was shooting on the higher moors and perhaps expeditions to neigh-bouring antiquities and spectacular viewpoints. Dinners no doubt were of a solid no-nonsense northern variety (For the royal visit, Armstrong brought in London caterers approved by the Prince of Wales, who was served

with his favourite champagne by waiters from Gunters used to waiting on him'.) Afterwards, there would have been conversation and cards, or the opportunities provided by the excellent modern library.

At the time of the royal visit there was no smoking room, and a watercolour records, probably correctly, that in summer at least the men could smoke on the garden terrace. Later in life Armstrong added a billiard room for the amusement of his younger relatives, and a small 'Electrical Room' where he could conduct his experiments without domestic disturbance. In summer the royal party would have had little

*Cragside is lit up for the royal visit*

'The château itself was a blaze of light. From every window the bright rays of the electric lamps shone with purest radiance, and the main front was made brilliant by a general illumination.'

*Newcastle Daily Journal*, 1884

## Menu for the royal dinner, 19 August 1884

HORS D'OEUVRES
*Huîtres au Naturel* (Oysters)

POTAGES (Soups)
*Tortue Claire* (Clear turtle)
*Crème de Volaille à la Princesse* (Cream of chicken)

POISSONS (Fish)
*Turbots farcis à la Normande* (Stuffed turbot braised in white wine)
*Rougets à l'Italienne* (Red mullet sautéed in butter and served in sauce)

ENTRÉES
*Coquilles de Foie Gras à la Strasbourg* (Scallops of Strasbourg pâté de foie gras)
*Côtelettes d'Agneau à la Piccolomini* (Lamb chops)

RELEVÉS
*Poulardes à la Montmorency* (Fowl with cherries)
*Jambon au Vin de Madère* (Ham in Madeira)
*Hanche de Venaison rôtie* (Roast haunch of venison)

RÔT (Roast)
*Grouse*
*Tomates à l'Espagnole* (tomatoes)

ENTREMETS
*Gelée de Marasquin aux Pêches* (Peaches in maraschino jelly)
*Poudings à la Vénitienne* (Cakes filled with pistachio ice-cream and decorated with raspberry ice)
*Soufflé glacé au Chocolat* (Iced chocolate soufflé)
*Talmouses à la Sefton* (Marzipan turnovers)

GLACES (Ices)
*Brown Bread Cream*
*Raspberry and Currant Water*

## Seating plan

| | | |
|---|---|---|
| Mr Howard | | Mr Knollys |
| Mrs Cadogan | | Mrs Watson |
| Lord Colville | | Lord Hastings |
| Mrs Wilberforce | | Miss Knollys |
| Duke of Sutherland | | Bishop of Newcastle |
| Lady Hastings | | Lady Armstrong |
| Princess of Wales | | Prince of Wales |
| Sir Wm. Armstrong | | Mrs Grey |
| Prince Albert Victor | | Prince George |
| Miss Cadogan | | Sir E. Grey |
| Mr Spencer | | Mr Calcraft |
| Colonel Clarke | | Mr W. Watson |

concern for the extremes of the Northumbrian climate. Winter visitors would have enjoyed not just the fires in most rooms, but also the central heating provided from two cavernous heating chambers below the house. Close by, there were also Turkish baths, which must have been particularly appreciated by oriental guests.

Armstrong was aware that, while Cragside was a comfortable home, it could also be an effective shop window for his guests. One may wonder how clients' decisions on the purchase of armaments were influenced by the hospitality at Cragside, how often marmalade was exchanged for battleships over breakfast.

*(Right) Armstrong reads the newspaper in his slippers in the Dining Room inglenook. The house was designed for informal weekend parties*

*(Left) The Prince of Wales smokes a cigar on the terrace during the royal visit of 1884. Armstrong (in black top hat) is seated opposite him*

# The House

## Building Cragside

Originally, the house was not intended to be large. As first built, from 1863, it was about the size of a comfortable detached villa in Jesmond or Gosforth or any of the well-to-do suburbs of Victorian England, and it was used for occasional sporting weekends. With the extension of the Northumberland Central Railway to Rothbury, projected in 1869, the vision for the house changed and, gradually, Cragside became the Armstrongs' main home. After Richard Norman Shaw first appeared in 1869, the house was subject to a series of extensions which lasted fifteen years. Additions (look out for dates on chimney stacks) were made to the north, then east, and then south – and upwards and, where the ground allowed, downwards as well. Even after Shaw's time (his last work on the house seems to have been in 1884), further extensions were made to the east until the house all but filled the quarry from which much of the building stone was taken.

In style, Shaw transformed an unpretentious, though resolutely irregular, house into a grand evocation of England's manorial past. He used unadorned timber and stone in the Arts-and-Crafts fashion of the time. He adopted many medieval features – mullioned windows, battlements, decorated barge boards, shouldered gables, steep roofs and clustered chimneys – but he used them in his own distinctive way.

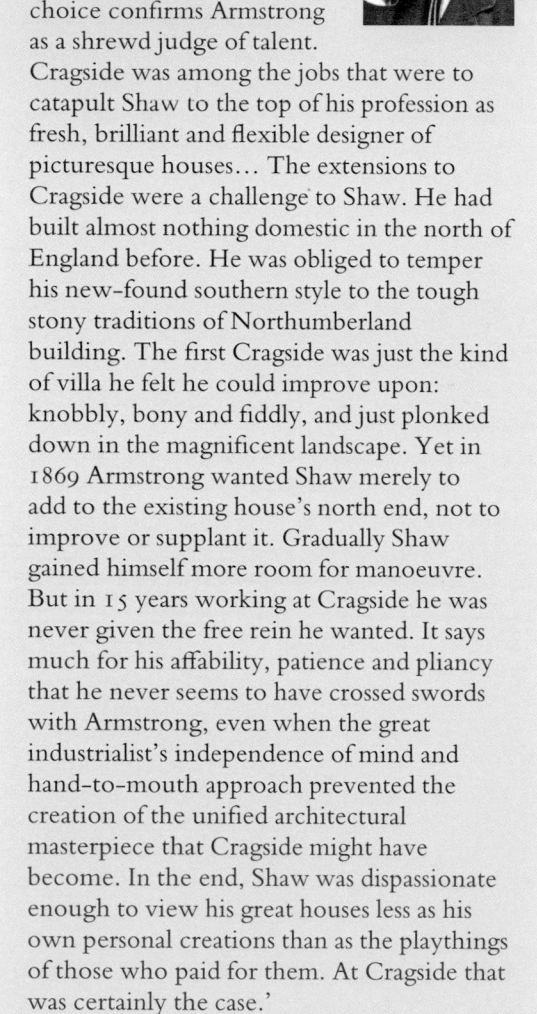

### The architect of Cragside

'The London architect upon whom Armstrong called to extend Cragside in 1869, Richard Norman Shaw (1831–1912), was not then well known. The choice confirms Armstrong as a shrewd judge of talent. Cragside was among the jobs that were to catapult Shaw to the top of his profession as fresh, brilliant and flexible designer of picturesque houses… The extensions to Cragside were a challenge to Shaw. He had built almost nothing domestic in the north of England before. He was obliged to temper his new-found southern style to the tough stony traditions of Northumberland building. The first Cragside was just the kind of villa he felt he could improve upon: knobbly, bony and fiddly, and just plonked down in the magnificent landscape. Yet in 1869 Armstrong wanted Shaw merely to add to the existing house's north end, not to improve or supplant it. Gradually Shaw gained himself more room for manoeuvre. But in 15 years working at Cragside he was never given the free rein he wanted. It says much for his affability, patience and pliancy that he never seems to have crossed swords with Armstrong, even when the great industrialist's independence of mind and hand-to-mouth approach prevented the creation of the unified architectural masterpiece that Cragside might have become. In the end, Shaw was dispassionate enough to view his great houses less as his own personal creations than as the playthings of those who paid for them. At Cragside that was certainly the case.'

Andrew Saint, biographer of Norman Shaw

*(Left) Cragside in the mid-1860s, before it had been transformed by Norman Shaw*

(*Above*) The entrance front today

(*Right*) A sketch by Norman Shaw
of Cragside's complex roofscape

'It will be very
satisfactory working
for Sir William as he
knows right well what
he is about'.
Richard Norman Shaw,
in a letter to his wife, 1869

# Tour of the House

## The Kitchen and Servants' Quarters

### Working at Cragside

It must have been regarded as a privilege to be part of the staff at Cragside. It was certainly better to work here than many places: the house was unusually warm and secure, food seems to have been plentiful and varied, and with its many patent labour-saving gadgets the house had more than a little novelty and interest. No doubt the servants were kept busy with all the routine tasks needed to maintain the household, but they must have been encouraged to realise that at least part of their master's inventive mind was directed to increasing efficiency and removing drudgery from their lives.

The Kitchen and the Sculleries beneath were the main focus for innovations. A Barker's mill (something like a lawn spray) turned the spits in front of the range. A 'dumb-waiter' lift was used to carry stores and equipment to and from the Kitchen. Electric bells could summon servants, but there were also electric gongs to summon guests to meals. There was even a primitive washing-up machine.

## Summoned by bells

The Butler, controlling all, had his day room strategically placed between the family rooms and the servants' areas. He was also in easy reach of the front door to supervise arrivals and departures. The Housekeeper and Cook each had their separate domains. For the younger ones there would have been much to learn. What was kept in all those cupboards? Bells ruled their world, regulating the day, indicating summonses from residents, and announcing arrivals. The Kitchen would have been always busy with preparations. Produce arrived from the gardens: vegetables, fruit and honey; there would also have been potted plants, cut flowers and foliage for decoration. From further afield, either from Rothbury or one of the estate farms, would have come meats, butter and cheeses, poultry, eggs, and game. From the Scullery, larders and cellar storage stretched underneath most of the courtyard. At this level, too, were the boilers which power the central heating systems, and the fuel stores.

### The ideal Victorian kitchen

'Light in abundance is most important; a side-light ought to flank the range rather than to face it, and if it can be placed on the cook's left hand, when working over the fire, this is highly appreciated.

'Coolness is a thing to be considered, for two reasons; first that the unpleasantness of the fire heat may not be intensified, and secondly that the air may not be needlessly tainted.

'The Aspect of wall-windows ought therefore to be Northward or Eastward, never Southward or Westward. Any ceiling-light ought to be so placed as to avoid hot sunshine. To make a Kitchen especially lofty (two stories in one for important cases) becomes almost a means to the same end. The roofing, it need scarcely be said, ought not to admit the heat and sunshine.'

Robert Kerr, *The Gentleman's House*, 1864

*(Left)*
*The Kitchen has a high ceiling and windows facing north and east to keep it cool, as Robert Kerr recommended*

*(Right)*
*The Butler's Pantry*

*The Scullery*

*Copper pans in the Kitchen*

## Lightening the load

The greatest blessing to the servants (and clearly placed primarily for their use rather than that of the guests) was a hydraulic lift, which could be used for carrying coal to all the upstairs rooms. Although running water was available in some parts of the house, the lift could also be used to get warming pans, water jugs, basins and other sanitary china to and from the bedrooms. Such practicalities were organised by the Housekeeper, who was also responsible for keeping rooms clean and providing a washing service, using the estate laundry at Tumbleton. Because of the lift, loaded linen baskets did not have to be carried up and down stairs.

## Separate spheres

The servants also had their own rooms. To the south of the Kitchen, next to the court-yard door, was their dining or common

## Loyal service

The Armstrongs were not merely good employers, but had an ability to inspire real loyalty. At the time of Lord Armstrong's death in 1900, William Avery, the head gamekeeper, had been at Cragside for 25 years; Henry Hudson, the head gardener, for 35 years; and

William Crosby, foreman workman, had served 37 years. Even more remarkable were Willie Mavin, the mason, who had been part of the building team which started the original house in 1863, and William Bertram, Armstrong's estate manager, who, with his wife, had shared with the Armstrongs the old miller's cottage at Burnfoot, when the house and its plantings were first planned. All of these continued to serve Lord Armstrong's great-nephew after 1900.

### The household staff in 1881

|  |  |  | per annum |
|---|---|---|---|
| Joseph Grey | Butler | 63 | £50 |
| Jane Eliott | Cook | 21 | £18 |
| Mary Ann Lawson | Housemaid | 20 | £14 |
| Mary Thompson | Housemaid | 20 | £13 |
| Jane Carr | Laundrymaid | 20 | £20 |
| Margaret Thompson | Dairymaid | 26 | £20 |
| Matilda Jeavers | Kitchenmaid | 17 | £14 |
| Anne Crozier | Dressmaker | 16 | £10 |

room, with the Housekeeper's sitting room above. With access firmly supervised by the Housekeeper, the maidservants' bedrooms took up space in the central tower (which was built mainly for external architectural effect, for there were no family rooms there). Men servants were kept safely isolated in the North Tower and the north-east wing, with their own separate external access from the courtyard. Many books in the house are marked 'Servants Room', suggesting that, in what little spare time they had, servants were encouraged to read. This accorded with Armstrong's provision of reading rooms and schools at Elswick.

*The household staff in 1886. Labour-saving gadgets made the servants' life less hard than elsewhere*

# The Dining Room

The Dining Room is one of two main rooms on the ground floor designed and decorated in his 'Old English' manner by Norman Shaw as part of his first additions to the house in 1870–2. They survive in good condition and are among the finest remaining Victorian domestic interiors in England. The effect is intended to be both homely and impressive. The room is panelled with light oak to high dado height (1.5 metres). There is a broad *bay window* on the north side (Ruskin stipulated that main rooms should have bows or bays), and facing this a splendid *side-board* recessed between doorways. The upper walls have *wallpaper* in two shades of green, specially made to resemble the original paper supplied by Cowtan's of London in 1872.

## Fireplace

The climax of the room is the stone inglenook. Its broad Gothic arch is elaborately carved, like the panelling, with decorative plants and animals. The heavy apron screen beneath the arch, with its deep stones checked into their neighbours for stability, is bor-rowed from the medieval kitchen of Fountains Abbey in Yorkshire, which Shaw had sketched in 1861. The fireplace itself is framed with coloured marbles and tiles and massive capitals, carved with cocks and wolves, supporting a lintel cosily inscribed 'East or West Hame's Best'. At each side of the inglenook is a heavy oak *settle*. Their fine carving, including the circular motifs (which Shaw designed and called 'pies'), must be the work of James Forsyth, Shaw's favourite craftsman, who produced the rest of the carving in the room.

## Pictures

It was sitting on one of these settles, with his dogs about him, that Lord Armstrong chose to be portrayed by Henry Emmerson

in 1880. The portrait is in the room (he is depicted with a bell-push on the extreme left in the panelling, showing that by then electricity had been brought into the room). He sits in an attitude which allows him to be reading when posing – a combination of informality and activity which typified the man. Portraits of Lord Armstrong's parents flank the fireplace. Opposite the fire is his sister, Anne, and beyond on horseback, her grandson, William Watson-Armstrong, who succeeded his great-uncle at Cragside in 1900.

## Movable feasts

Curiously, there are two *dining tables*, which are clearly shown in a photograph of the room in 1881. Perhaps the Armstrongs liked the option of eating in the window (at breakfast?) or in front of the fire (in chillier weather?). From a technical point of view, the circular 'Capstan' table would certainly have appealed to Armstrong. Taken from a design of about 1835 by Robert Jupe, the table has removable segments so that it can be made to seat more or fewer guests.

## Stained glass for all seasons

The stained glass in the windows of the inglenook was designed by William Morris and supplied in 1873. Four Seasons (autumn is illustrated here), represent the Four young women, each suitably attired. Norman Shaw would have been keen to introduce fine craftsmanship to enhance the medieval qualities of his building. Armstrong, for his part, probably needed little persuasion: he had already used some of the earliest Morris wallpaper in the original house. Morris involved his friends, members and associates of the Pre-Raphaelite Brotherhood, in design. There is more Morris glass to be seen in the Library, Upper Stairs and Gallery, including designs by Ford Madox Brown, Dante Gabriel Rossetti, Edward Burne-Jones and Philip Webb.

*(Left) The inglenook fireplace*

*(Left) The fireplace
surround combines
Egyptian onyx,
red marble and
blue majolica tiles*

# The Library

The Library, completed in 1872, was part of Norman Shaw's first addition to the original house. Placed adjoining the Dining Room, it was originally used as a drawing room. When the new Drawing Room was completed in 1884, this room, which contains a good proportion of the books in the house, became known as the Library. The books, however, are not dominant; indeed they are barely apparent at all to a visitor entering the room for the first time. With its light atmosphere, comfortable furnishings, warm colouring and, not least, the lovely views into the valley, it was the family's favourite living room.

The Library's light oak *panelling*, elaborately carved by James Forsyth, is really a tall dado reaching almost half way up the walls. The *chimneypiece* has an improbable combination of wide areas of plain onyx (probably a souvenir of Armstrong's visit to Egypt in 1872) framed in Emperor's red marble and all embracing bright blue majolica tile cheeks with figures from a design of 1853 by Alfred Stevens. The upper walls are covered in embossed paper, snuff-coloured to enhance the display of pictures. The beamed and coffered ceiling, again by Forsyth, includes walnut panels set in squares with confidently carved bosses, and its cornice compartments are painted with branches and leaves set on a gold ground.

'The Library is a fascinating essay in the application of Shaw's essentially masculine 'Old English' style to a room requiring delicacy of treatment.'

Andrew Saint

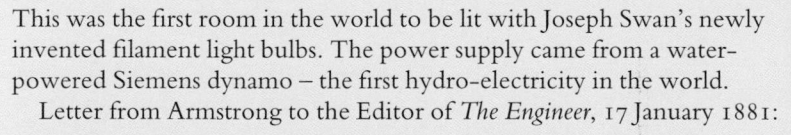

### First light

This was the first room in the world to be lit with Joseph Swan's newly invented filament light bulbs. The power supply came from a water-powered Siemens dynamo – the first hydro-electricity in the world.

Letter from Armstrong to the Editor of *The Engineer*, 17 January 1881:

'The Library, which is a room of 33 feet by 20 feet with a large recess on one side, is well lighted by eight lamps. Four are clustered in one globe of ground glass, suspended from the ceiling of the recess, and the remainder are placed singly in globes, in various parts of the room, upon vases…. These vases, being enamel on copper, are themselves conductors, and serve for carrying the return current from the incandescent carbon to a metallic case in connection with the main return wire. The entering current is brought by a branch wire to a small insulated mercury cup in the centre of the base, and is carried forward to the lamp by a piece of insulated wire which passes through the interior to the lamp on the top. The protruding end of this wire is naked, and dips into the mercury cup when the vase is set down. Thus the lamp may be extinguished and relighted at pleasure merely by removing the vase from its seat or setting it down again.'

## Stained glass

The upper sections of the bay window have stained glass supplied by Morris & Co. Each of the outer four (suitable to a library) has a pair of authors: Homer and Aeschylus, Virgil and Horace, Dante and Chaucer, all designed by Burne-Jones, and Spenser and Milton by Madox Brown. The six middle panels, designed by Rossetti, give a lively version of the life of St George and the troublesome dragon.

## Furnishings

The light woodwork sets off the prevailing red-brown and black tones of the furnishings. The fitted *carpet* seems to have been an original feature (it was certainly there by 1891) and is another example of Cragside being in the vanguard of domestic furnishing. Its red-brown colour, uniting with those of the curtains and leather sofas, gives the room a welcoming warmth. In contrast, the room has a fine set of dark *furniture*, including an outstanding set of chairs in the delicate 'Queen Anne' style made of ebonised mahogany with cane seats and gilded leather backs. Made by Gillows of Lancaster, apparently to designs by Shaw, they also reflect the fashion for Japanese taste in the 1870s.

## Pictures

The pictures are a mixture (as they seem to have been in Armstrong's time) of family portraits, copies of Old Masters, and more up-to-date works by local artists. The greatest loss to Cragside was the sale in 1910 of many of the house's pictures by outstanding 19th-century artists, but the remaining pictures still give an idea of the Armstrongs' taste for landscape (especially with coasts, lakes, mills and other watery associations), historical subjects, and more sentimental pictures, usually of children – reflecting perhaps the unmentioned sadness that the Armstrongs had no children of their own.

Armstrong did not neglect local artists, and some are represented here. There is a *Coastal*

*Scene with Fishing Boats near Flamborough* of *c.*1840 by Thomas Miles Richardson, who, through his academy in Newcastle, fostered development of the visual arts in the north-east. John Wilson Carmichael, represented by an atmospheric *Coastal Scene by Moonlight* (1840), moved from Newcastle to London and gained a national reputation as a marine painter. Bernard Benedict Hemy's *Sailing Ship towed by a Tug* (*c.*1880) is typical of his Tyne scenes. More relevant to Cragside is the large view above the chimneypiece by his brother, Thomas Hemy, of *Elswick Works on the Tyne* (*c.*1880), which shows Armstrong's engineering works as it approached the height of its fame.

Perhaps the picture which most typifies the Armstrongs' taste, with its Pre-Raphaelite colouring and detail and its gentle sentimentality, is Raphael Sorbi's *Italian Girl with Doves* (1866), which Armstrong purchased in 1869.

*A flight of steps down from the Library lobby leads to the Turkish Baths.*

*(Right) The ornate metal hanging lampshades were supplied by Lea, Sons & Co. of Shrewsbury before 1895. The firm's illustrated catalogue from which they were ordered is still in the house*

*(Opposite) The oak Library bookcases*

## The Turkish Baths

The suite of rooms includes a steam bath, a cold plunge, a hot bath and a shower, as well as water closets and a changing room. They are the lowest and the first completed part of Norman Shaw's first addition to the original house. His plan, which shows that modifications were still being made, is dated 5 May 1870, and Armstrong's friend, Thomas Sopwith, recorded in his diary that 'the Turkish Bath at Cragside was used for the first time on November 4th 1870'.

The baths were part of Lord Armstrong's innovative provision of central heating for the whole house. The space occupied by the baths is cleverly situated between chambers with huge water-pipe coils, which, heated from the boiler to the north, were the source of hot air that was ducted up into the main house. Meanwhile, the baths are warmed through the walls on two sides, and guests, particularly those from the Orient accustomed to elaborate bathing, could be made to feel at home. Armstrong, who was always keen to build up foreign business, seems to have taken the pragmatic view that Chinese or Burmese or Japanese arms ministers would be more likely to agree to handsome contracts, if they were both well entertained and comfortable – even in a Northumbrian winter. The ploy seems to have been successful. Armstrong was showered in return with orders and honours.

*Back at ground-floor level, a corridor lined with a dado of majolica tiles leads past three small rooms from the original house to the stairs.*

## The Japanese Room

It contains gifts and mementoes of the Armstrongs' friendship with the Tokugawa family, which spanned three generations. The room is dedicated to Yorisada Tokugawa, 'Friend of Humanity', an

*At the head of the stairs is the Boudoir.*

The **crouching beasts** on the newel posts held some of the original light fittings with curled tops rather like fishing rods under strain. The present ragged staffs supporting beacon baskets were substituted before 1895. At the foot of the Main Stairs is a drawing and the only photo of the original 1863 house.

**Sculpture**

In a niche is *The Slave Girl*, sculpted by John Bell. It dates from 1870, when the American Civil War and the publication of *Uncle Tom's Cabin* had sharpened awareness of the plight of slaves. In an attempt to reflect this mood, Bell created a figure which was popular at the time, but may be uncomfortable to modern eyes.

*Distinguished visitors*

Most notable among Cragside's distinguished Japanese visitors have been the present Emperor (when Crown Prince) in 1953, and his son, the present Crown Prince, in 1991.

uncle of the Empress of Japan who gave the fine set of prints to the Armstrongs just after the First World War.

## The Garden Alcove

This was the usual access to the Rock Gardens (see p. 34).

## The Study

This room began life as Lady Armstrong's sitting room and later became her husband's study. One of his *microscopes* is displayed on the desk. The *portrait* of Lord Armstrong at the age of 21 by James Ramsay is generously loaned by Alvis Vickers plc.

## The Stair Hall

The Stair Hall is an inner extension of the Entrance Hall in roughly the same place as the stairs of the first house, but enlarged, panelled and adorned with portraits and hunting trophies.

*(Above left) The Turkish Baths*

*(Left) A Japanese actor, print by Utamaro (Japanese Room)*

*(Right) The heraldic beasts on the newel posts in the Stair Hall support electric light fittings in the form of beacon baskets*

# The Red Bedroom and Dressing Room

They were part of the first extension to the house. They retain the mid-20th-century *wallpaper* which was put up when great conifers in the Rock Gardens started making the rooms dark. From here there is a good view across the Rock Gardens to the Iron Bridge and waterfalls along Debdon Burn.

in the house, one dated 1864. The papers here were reprinted using the original 1864 blocks.

# The Boudoir

This was the upstairs sitting room of the 1863 house. Its compartmental *ceiling* has stencilled patterns and gilding of about 1880. This was uncovered and the original Cowtan paper of 1866 replicated in 1978. The set of satinwood *furniture* of the 1880s is on loan from the Victoria & Albert Museum

# The Yellow and White Bedrooms

They have some of the earliest William Morris *wallpapers*, 'Fruit' and 'Bird and Trellis' respectively. Fragments of both were found

# The Morning Room

Known to later generations as 'Mother's Room', it was an upstairs drawing room, a private retreat. Carved on the oak door in Latin is a rather forbidding warning, meaning 'it is not those who ask but those who are asked that I admit'. The room was restored in 1987–8 (funded by the County Durham Centre of the National Trust) to its appearance almost a century earlier (see the old photographs displayed in the room) with patterned wallpaper, painted ceiling paper, light brackets and a floral carpet. Most of the *furniture* here is original, a mixture of provincial comfort and delicate display pieces of the 'Sheraton revival'.

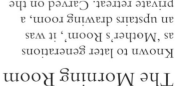

*(Left) The Yellow Bedroom*
*(Right) The Morning Room*

# The Bamboo Room

This was another example of Japanese taste, though the wood is not bamboo, but carved and painted to look like it. Were oriental guests flattered by it or just puzzled?

# The Armstrong Room

The former Brown Bedroom provides opportunities for visitors to sit, or read, or discover more about Lord Armstrong and Cragside.

# The Bathroom

The adjacent room was added to the house about 1900. Early *wallpaper* was revealed during repair works in 2006. A well-preserved section depicting bird silhouettes in blue and red squares has been left exposed.

*The Bamboo Room*

# The Gallery

The Gallery was the largest room in the second major extension of the house, of 1873–4, which created a new south front. It was also the first room to be lit with electricity – in this case with arc lamps in 1878. These must have given gatherings a strange ghostly atmosphere; anyway, this type of lighting was considered unacceptable, and twenty of Joseph Swan's bulbs were substituted two years later. Lord Armstrong recalled that the room served as a sitting room, but, after the further extension of the house and the addition of the present Drawing Room, it became a gallery for pictures and sculpture.

## Pictures

The pictures along the long walls are by Henry Hetherington Emmerson (1831–95), a favourite artist of the Armstrongs, whose local historical scenes and fancy pictures, dear to Victorian taste, were laden with sentimentality, gloom or death (or all three). The worst culprits are *Orphan of the Storm* of 1875, a bleak winter scene with a lamb beside its dead mother, and *Faithful unto Death* of 1874; in this enormous pastel Emmerson makes the most of a local tragedy in which a shepherd died in a blizzard. The unfortunate man lies on his back, his face grey with frost, while his anxious collies howl and snuffle, but will not leave.

Altogether more bracing is *Gilnockie Tower in 1530*, painted in 1880. Lord Armstrong, in search of ancestry, implied some kinship with Johnnie Armstrong of Gilnockie, a notorious reiver who has a prominent place in border ballads. Emmerson's depiction of the tower was based on the original, which survives near Langholm. Its name was also adopted for Cragside's south-east tower, which Armstrong built originally as an observatory. Johnnie Armstrong and his

When first built, the Gallery was designated simply as 'museum' and intended as a private place for Armstrong to study and to keep his scientific, geological and natural history specimens. At that stage it gave access to only the Gilnockie Tower and Armstrong's observatory. Gradually, the space was transformed into a gallery; south windows were blocked, and northern roof lights improved. With the building of the Drawing Room in 1884, the Gallery became a rather superior passage, part of a grand progress towards the house's most important room. Even so, the space has never quite lost its museum atmosphere. Armstrong's cabinets of geological samples are still here. So, too, are some fine examples of taxidermy. These are the work of John Hancock, the celebrated local naturalist whose pioneering work in mounting specimens in natural attitudes (including examples of 'nature red in tooth and claw') shocked and thrilled mid-Victorians. Hancock and Armstrong were friends, and Armstrong contributed liberally to the establishment of the Newcastle Museum of Natural History, which was eventually named after Hancock.

companions are shown returning triumphant with stolen stock. The sting in the tale is that within a few weeks he and 48 of his clan, tricked into attending a muster at Hawick, were executed on the orders of James V.

## The Watercolour Gallery

A smaller room to the north was used as a watercolour gallery. Included here are works by Thomas Girtin, Clarkson Stanfield, Frederick Goodall, E. W. Cooke and T. M. Richardson. Here, too, is an elaborately decorated book of watercolours by H. H. Emmerson and J. T. Dixon, which was presented to the Armstrongs by the people of Rothbury to commemorate the royal visit of 1884.

*Up a short stair at the west end of the Gallery is the Owl Suite.*

## The Owl Suite

This was specially refurnished for the royal visit with distinctive furniture and in-built plumbing. The previous use of these rooms is not recorded. This may be for a good reason. There must have been a deal of covert snobbish and jealous comment about the Armstrongs (then mere commoners) being accorded the honour of royal residence. If, as seems likely, the main room had served as a billiard and smoking room, it might have been awkward to explain that it had been converted for the reception of princes and princesses. Anyway, the visit was regarded as a great success by all.

The most notable features are the *beds* with their distinctive posts with owl finials. Designed by Norman Shaw, they were made from American black walnut probably by W. H. Lascelles. Two, the largest and smallest, have always been in the house (though the larger had to be re-assembled in 1979). The middle one was generously returned to Cragside from a farm in Leicestershire in 2006, having been brought there from Cheshire a generation ago.

# The Drawing Room

Norman Shaw's last, and largest, extension to the house was completed just in time for the royal visit of 1884. The style is no longer 'Olde English', but Classical Renaissance and is typical of Shaw's more opulent interiors of the 1880s. The scheme probably owes much to Shaw's brilliant chief assistant at that time, William Lethaby. Above the panelled dado the walls are covered with deep red wool damask. The cove of the ceiling is occupied by massive plaster panels, which curve up to the central skylight, the only source of natural light apart from one window in the south-west corner, set deep in a bay carved from Cragside stone.

The completion of the Drawing Room, by far the largest room in the house, marks a change in Cragside's status. The house had long ceased to be a small fishing lodge, but, as it grew, it had retained a comfortable informality. The Drawing Room, with its long approach

## For show, not warmth

The *chimneypiece*, extending across most of the south wall, projects into the room with crushing confidence. It was designed in the early Renaissance classical style by William Lethaby, and carved by Farmer and Brindley. Two columns seem to bulge, and, above, pairs of putti (young boys) fidget under the weight of ten tons of carved and polished Italian marble. The space beneath, in front of the fire, is large enough for a dozen to meet (which occasionally they still do).

Because the room was built so far into the quarry, the smoke from the turf fire had to be ducted up to a separate chimney built higher up the hillside. The fire, in any case, was largely decorative, because this great space was heated from below by its own boiler and pipe system.

*(Left)*
*The Drawing Room*

through the Gallery provided a space for grand gatherings, for formality, and ostentation. It is no accident that it was rushed to completion just in time for the visit of the Prince and Princess of Wales. Despite protestations about the informality of the visit, it is doubtful whether it could have taken place without the Drawing Room. The Dining Room was barely big enough to sit 24, and a larger reception area was needed, and was used, during the visit. It would be a mistake, however, to suggest that the room was built expressly for the royal visit. Armstrong, who was no novice at public relations, must have recognised the potential for such an entertainment space just as he had in building, and then extending, the banqueting house near his home at Jesmond Dene. But the room is so large that it can hardly have been used comfortably on a daily basis. Such thoughts would not have been uppermost in Armstrong's mind in 1884, and we may imagine with what pride he conducted his royal guests to see this new room.

Of the later use of the room, little is known. While it would have been difficult to roll back the vast Axminster fitted carpet for dancing, there certainly would have been music, though the family Bechstein piano, and its patent pianola, were not acquired until 1901. Surviving photographs also show that the room was used in the early 20th century for celebratory dinners for large numbers of guests. Gradually, however, as resources dwindled, the room went out of regular use.

### Pictures

The present collection is a shadow of the original, much of which was sold in 1910. Nevertheless, most of the present pictures did belong to Armstrong, and in recent years it has been possible to repatriate a few of those that went astray.

Among the principal paintings now in the room are three portraits of the second Lady Armstrong and her children by Mary Lemon Waller on the north wall, J. M. W. Turner's *Cilgerran Castle*, E. W. Cooke's *Venetian Scene*, Walter Horsley's *The Water Seller*, T. M. Richardson's *Rountin Brig*, and Edward

*(Right) Undine; by Alexander Munro*

Patry's *Only an Orange Girl*, which escaped the sale only when it was discovered that it was not by Millais.

### Sculpture

Alexander Munro's *Undine* shows the water nymph who accidentally drowned her errant husband. The figure can be rotated on its stand, demonstrating Munro's virtuosity of technique and balance: the nymph's front foot barely touches the lilies.

## The Billiard Room and Electrical Room

The last major addition to Cragside, of 1895, was not designed by Norman Shaw, but by Frederick Waller of Gloucester, in a Jacobean revival style with panelling and classical columns. The billiard furniture was supplied by Burroughes & Watts. This is the most easterly extension of the house and built against the quarry face. The main light comes from a sky-light, though at the south end a bay window looks onto a small terrace cut into the hill slope.

This was largely a gentlemen's retreat, with military pictures, leather furniture and sombre decoration. Framed certificates, honours and awards, both here and in the corridor beyond, are reminders of Lord Armstrong's long and successful international career as well as some of his more local interests such as Rothbury church, where he served as a churchwarden.

The room was presumably built for the younger members of the family, though the extension included on the north side an Electrical Room (currently awaiting restoration to its original appearance). This was set aside from the bustle of the house so that Armstrong could pursue his scientific studies without disturbance. It was here that he conducted his last experiments.

# The Landscape

## Creating the estate

The Cragside landscape is so extensive and has now become so integrated with its surroundings that it is difficult to imagine that none of it existed 150 years ago. Its present glorious maturity, something that Armstrong could only imagine, we owe to his extraordinary foresight. His library shows that he was aware of gardening fashions and particularly of the division between formal areas and areas where plants were allowed to grow in their natural way. But while he was interested in the detail of gardening, he developed by reading, travel and observation a deep understanding of the wider landscape.

## Imagining the landscape

In 1855 Armstrong was encouraged by Mrs Rendell, the widow of his friend George Meadows Rendell, to write down one of the occasional yarns with which he used to amuse her sons when still boys. The result was

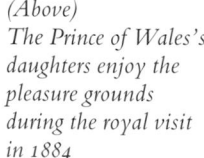

*(Above)*
*The Prince of Wales's daughters enjoy the pleasure grounds during the royal visit in 1884*

*(Left)*
*Cragside in the late 1870s, when Armstrong's massive planting programme was still in its early stages*

*The Traprocks of the Himalaya Mountains,* an improbable adventure set in a landscape of rocky mountains, dense forests, sweeping lakes and abundant coloured shrubs. One watercourse traps the hero, and another provides a means of daring escape. It is not important that Armstrong never saw the Himalayas; what matters about the story is that it shows his ability to imagine great landscapes and to understand how the constituent parts combine to create the whole. It was a talent which he used in his own gardening, first at Jesmond, and then on a much grander scale at Cragside.

In satisfying his typically Victorian wish to collect and categorise nature, Armstrong was supported by his wife, and a huge amount was also owed to Henry Hudson, Head Gardener from the 1870s, who combined the professional plantsman's expertise with an ability to manage a large team of men, first creating, and then maintaining, the gardens.

The Armstrongs were happy to share their gardens. The grounds were open every Thursday throughout the year, and on Sundays by special ticket. Visitors were welcome to walk and wonder.

## *Cragside in 1881*

'Imagine a great hill covered from bottom to crest with huge grey boulder stones, and half way up, cut out of a steppe on the hill side, the site and placing of a building of the most picturesque kind imaginable. Then having chosen the site and placed the house, call forth your gardeners by the hundreds, and bid them make amongst and around those crags and boulders cunningly winding walks, every one formed of steps of the natural grey stone. Then bring your evergreens and rare heather by the tens of thousands, plant them over and about the place till there is hardly a spot of bare soil left; then with the rarest and commonest ferns plant every crevice amongst the boulders. Form two artificial lakes in the valley near the house, so that you can defy suspicion of the manufacture. Make a carriage approach from opposite ends of the valley, so easy and pleasant that it might be transplanted from Hyde Park; and, beside these, let there be rolling along the hill, at two heights above, carriage drives that for views and healthful breezes shall be immaculate. Along the valley let there be a brooklet teeming with fish, and covered and bordered with trees and rocks forming a veritable glen: span the stream by rustic and iron bridges, which form the centres of a score of perfect pictures.'

T. Raffles Davison in *The British Architect*, May 1881

## *Cragside in 1906*

'Perhaps the most striking season is the spring, when the azaleas are out and the rhododendra in full bloom, growing in their thousands right on the hillside, their beauty much emphasised by the huge boulders amongst which they flourish. There are five lochs on the estate, which gleam like silver mirrors framed in with jewels, masses of double sweet-scented gorse, weigelias, calmias, Alpine roses, and thousands of rock plants, in addition to the large plantations of coniferae &c. It is calculated that, taking in the forest plantations and the 500 acres of ornamental planting, about 1,400 acres have been covered, and not less than ten to twelve millions of trees and plants have been used. Practically not a tree or shrub has perished, testifying to Lord Armstrong's care in his first choice of plants, which he knew would be congenial to the soil, and, secondly, to the manner of planting trees. He was well rewarded for this care and patience. He took the keenest interest in the work, every detail being submitted to him. The late Lady Armstrong was often up and round the estate at six in the morning, in order to see his wishes were carried out, and the whole work was ably superintended by Mr. William Bertram, steward to the estate.'

Winny, Lady Armstrong, August 1906

# Tour of the Garden

## The Rock Gardens

Rock gardens became important from the 1860s, being closely linked with the introduction of alpine plants to Britain. They developed towards an increasingly natural look. Those at Cragside are one of the wonders of English gardening. They are massive and bold in the fashion of the time but in both extent and diversity they have no obvious rivals. They cover almost two hectares and for decades had been largely hidden under a cloak of *Gaultheria shallon* and *Rhododendron ponticum*. Gradually, they have been revealed and restored; work began (with one gardener!) in 1988 and still continues.

Looking at the great 'rockscapes' today, it is difficult to believe that almost all the stones around the house had to be manoeuvred into position by men using only levers and blocks and tackle. Unlike some Victorian gardens which copied real rock outcrops in Britain and abroad, those at Cragside took their character from the immediate locality, from the crags above the Coquet River and the Debdon Burn which gave the house its name. Fell sandstone was brought in from the surrounding moors and placed to show its weathered sides.

There are three main areas with distinct types of rockwork. The oldest, of the 1870s, north and west of the house, is the most unusual, where a 'tumbling' effect was used to create a giant scree. This may be the last surviving example of its type on such a grand scale. Closer to the house on its west side, rocks are laid as a grand pavement, and this system was used again around 1890 to the east of the carriage circle at the front door. There, too, a large band of exposed bedrock

*(Right) The Rock Gardens are planted with purple and white heathers and other alpines*

was extended upwards with strata-style rock-work. Close examination is needed to see where the natural rock ends and the garden rockwork begins.

Cascades were included in the design to the north of the house and in the western scree to introduce movement and the sound of water. There is even an echo chamber – a hollowed cave behind one of the falls to enhance the sound. On the lowest western slope the lower

cascade had been lost in landslips caused by flooding and erosion in Debdon Burn. The cascade was rebuilt in 2006 following extensive repair works to the burn banks and waterfalls. This process showed that much concrete had been used originally to secure features along the water courses.

The replanting is balanced to avoid covering too much rock. Heathers and heaths (8,000 in total) have been reintroduced in the west garden. On the large western banks are plantings of both evergreen and deciduous azaleas mixed with other shrubs such as species of Berberis, Sorbus, Pieris and Vaccinium. More robust alpine species grow among the smaller outcrops. The south rock garden has a different character, with plantings from warmer parts of Europe and New Zealand. Elsewhere on the estate, natural outcrops remain in position, sometimes with additions, and sometimes blasted away to give access for a drive or footpath.

*(Above and right)  The Rock Gardens*

## The Pinetum

A tree collection, known as an arboretum or pinetum depending on the selected species, was regarded as a symbol of wealth and status in Victorian England. To some extent they were seen as a reflection of the global prestige of the British Empire. The activities of plant hunters all over the world made it possible to have such collections at home. The Cragside collection concentrated on coniferous (cone-bearing) trees and especially those from North America. Once the Armstrongs started to plant trees, it seems, they saw no reason to stop. Towards the end of the 19th century it was calculated that they had planted over seven million trees and shrubs, and at one stage as many as 150 people were employed upon the estate. According to one tradition, Lady Armstrong paid local people a penny a bucket to bring rich valley soil up from the Coquet valley to help plants get established among the moorland rocks and upland storms.

*(Left) The Pinetum*

Young trees have been planted to provide long-term balance and to ensure that areas of original trees do not all mature and die around the same time. Storms caused losses in 1998 and 2001, but this opened areas for replanting. Many of the trees are labelled; some are 'champions', the largest known of their species in England. With the removal of aggressive weeds and thick undergrowth, the floor of the Pinetum has been taken back to grass, allowing the planting of both native and exotic bulbs and perennials to form a spring meadow.

## The Valley Garden

The Valley Garden occupies the main views from the house, and centres on the Iron Bridge, from which there are lovely views both up and down Debdon Burn: upstream to a series of waterfalls beneath towering Douglas firs; and downstream towards the house, set at the top of its rock gardens with the great backdrop of trees rising behind.

During the 20th century the lower valley sides became densely entangled with unrestrained undergrowth beneath the trees. Gradually, this area is being transformed back to its original appearance, using plants from all over the world, and mixing exotic and native species. Upstream, the levels along the burn provide a contrasting opportunity to mix shrubs and robust herbaceous plants.

## The Iron Bridge

Dating from about 1875, this is itself a wonder in the way it sweeps across the valley with three light arches supported on two stone piers. Level with the foot of the main Rock Garden, it allowed access to the Formal Gardens without having to make the steep climb down to the burn and up the other side. The bridge was probably constructed at Armstrong's Elswick works on the Tyne and transported north in sections on the new railway. Although the carbon content of its wrought iron does not equate to that of modern steel, it is still significant and gives the iron added strength; it might be called 'proto-steel'. For safety reasons, the bridge has been closed to visitors since the 1970s. The original design was delicate, and unfortunate structural alterations, combined with lack of maintenance over the years, have resulted in some weaknesses. Nor was it originally intended to carry crowds. A restoration scheme is planned to repair the structure, give it greater strength, and so to return it to its original use.

## Tumbleton Lake

The valley is enclosed at the upper end by the dam which forms Tumbleton Lake. This is one of the five major lakes which were created on the estate.

Below the dam is the *Pump House*, which, by an ingenious set of opposite-displacement plunger pumps, used to supply water to the house.

*(Above, right)*
*The Iron Bridge*

*(Right)*
*The stables by*
*Tumbleton Lake*

## The Autumn Colour Walk

This links the Iron Bridge in the Valley Garden to the formal terraces. Always part of the enclosed ornamental garden, it anticipates, with glimpses of parkland and more distant hills, the spectacular wider views from the Formal Gardens. The restoration of this area, to reinforce the deciduous plantings, was initiated in memory of Sheila Pettit, who did so much to save Cragside. Acer, Sorbus, Rhus, Betula, Crataegus and Cotoneaster form the planting backbone, with beech, cherry and hornbeam beyond. The grass area is also very rich in wild flowers, which provide colour from the spring until cutting in the late summer.

A flight of great stone steps makes the final approach to the Formal Gardens and here the original planting drifts back into conifers and evergreens. The steps had become buried by undergrowth and leaf mould when the Formal Gardens were in separate ownership; but after the two areas were reunited in 1991, with a notable community effort, clearance was carried out by the local Cubs.

## The Formal Gardens

Armstrong's original purchase of land was in this area, where, unlike the steep sides of the Debdon valley, there had been small fields on a south-facing slope. The ground lent itself to terracing into three main levels, each with lovely views southwards over the Coquet valley. The rich alluvial soils allow the cultivation of a wide range of hardy and tender plants. This is very much an engineer's garden with a logical layout dominated by bold straight lines, no-nonsense joinery and ironwork, and massive, finely finished stonework paths, bed fenders and wall copings. The heavy construction has stood the test of time. Despite minor changes in the 1920s and 1980s, the basic Victorian framework survived, providing vital guidance to both building and planting restoration works.

This on-site evidence is the more important because of the lack of documentary evidence, though a good description of 1880 in *The Gardener's Journal* has provided a basis for restoration. The other vital source of information was the late Ken Davison, whose father had been Head Gardener after the First World War. He himself started as a gardener at Cragside in 1923 and retired as Head Gardener in 1980. Ken's memories, so freely given, provided vital links between the past and present.

## The Clock Tower

It was built in the late 1860s in a Gothic Revival style typical of the time. There are pointed windows, cross loops and cottage gables below a three-stage tower; this starts square, rises through an octagonal stage with four bulging circular clock faces, to an arcaded belfry with a pointed roof and weather vane. Both building and clock were restored in 1992.

The Clock Tower was both the estate time-piece and its pay office. The clock had two mechanisms, one for the clockworks and the other to strike the bell by which the estate was regulated. The bell sounded 24 times to start and finish work and at meal times. Its mechanism even allowed for different striking times on Saturdays and Sundays. At the peak of construction there were more than 300 people working at Cragside: gardeners, stone-masons,

### Beds for bugs

By providing bug boxes, avoiding the use of pesticides, and planting a wide range of nectar-rich plants, we attract many insects into the garden, including ladybirds and lacewings, which feed on thousands of aphids. Small, non-stinging mason bees lay their eggs in the hollow canes, plastering the ends with mud to keep their developing young safe from predators.

carpenters, gamekeepers and labourers, all working a twelve-hour day. Staff received their weekly pay from small numbered wooden boxes each about 10cm square. Under the watchful eye of William Bertram, the estate manager, this simple system ensured that all were properly paid.

## The Top Terrace

This was once dominated by a great glasshouse range, which was divided to provide a variety of environments: a great palm house, tropical and temperate ferneries, an orchid house, and a show house. The glass super-structures were demolished in the 1920s, but the walls on which they stood have survived, as has the elaborate rockwork in the two ferneries. The original divisions, now redefined with an open timber framework, are planted (for the summer) as if still glazed, with hardy and tender subjects to offer a conservatory experience – alas, without the conservatories. Plants from all over the world give some feeling of its original exotic character. One day it will be possible to restore the conservatories, and to bring back the spirit of the great plant-hunting age.

Beyond a screen wall to the west were potting sheds, stores and a bothy for the duty gardeners. A cart gate in the boundary wall gave access to the roadway and to the original kitchen gardens beyond.

*(Right) The Clock Tower*

## The Middle Terrace

This is a broad lawn with banks to east and south. On the most exposed corner where the two banks meet, Armstrong set his heliograph, or sun-recorder, on a stone pedestal. The lawn is ringed with important features: to the north the Orchard House and the Carpet Beds; to the west the Biennial Border; and at the foot of the southern bank the Dahlia Walk.

## The Orchard House

The largest surviving glasshouse dates from the 1870s. Its restoration began in 1992 and took over two years to complete. The building has three sections, the middle set forward and slightly taller than the wings. Built to provide shelter from the Northumberland climate for the cultivation of hardy and tender fruits, it had a boiler in the basement and an elaborate heating system. Two interior walls divide the inside

into three sections. In each there are large earthenware pots set on superb sandstone steps. Each pot sits on a turntable which allowed the pots to be turned to ensure even ripening and growth. This system seems to be unique to Cragside.

Replanting of the fruit trees began in 1995. The east wing has varieties of figs and grapes; the west wing has peaches and nectarines; and the centre has pears, mulberries, apricots, plums, gages, lemons, grapefruit, mandarins and oranges. It is intended that the Orchard House should reflect the glories of the Victorian fruit growers' high art of cultivation. The trees are all pre-1900 cultivars.

### Saving skills

Just as essential as the restoration of the buildings and historic plant collections is the need to maintain the skills of the past and for training to ensure that these are passed to future generations. If neglected, the importance of fine detail may be lost for ever.

*(Left)*
*The Orchard
House*

*(Right)*
*The Dahlia
Walk*

## Carpet bedding

Beside the Orchard House are two stone-framed
sloping beds designed for carpet bedding. Since
1993 they have been planted each year with
diminutive foliage plants arranged to create
intricate patterns. The design is different each
time and usually has some reference to the
Armstrong family, or a celebration or anniver-
sary. Once the plants are established, they are
clipped fortnightly, using sheep shears, to form a
neat flat surface with a carpet-like pattern.
Again, it is the survival of this art and craft of
designing, planting and clipping which is
important. While some pattern-planting
survives, notably in municipal gardens, this is
now almost always done with flowers. Foliage
carpet bedding is now very rare; indeed that at
Cragside may be a unique survival. Properly
done, it needs much of the gardeners' time.
Each bed takes 10,000 plants, and all have to be
raised in the nursery; and the arrangements only
span the summer. To provide spring colour,
the beds are planted in the autumn with tulips,
pansies and polyanthus.

*(Left)   Carpet bedding*

## The Biennial Border

Laid out beneath the wall to the west of the
lawn, this is also a rarity today. It provides
vibrant early summer colour, when the rest of
the Formal Garden changes from spring to
summer bedding. The plants store energy for a
year, and the following year expend it in a
magnificent floral display before they set seed
and die. As elsewhere in the Formal Gardens,
displays are changed each year and never
repeated. Biennials used here include hybrid
foxgloves, Canterbury bells, Siberian wall-
flowers, verbascums and lupins.

## The Dahlia Walk

Below the south bank, the Dahlia Walk was
restored in 1994, since when it has been planted
annually with 700 plants, giving a kaleidoscope
of colour in the autumn. Edge-planting of one
colour carries the eye along the borders, with
grouped plants behind giving bold blocks of
colour. The strident colouring of dahlias
appealed to the Victorians (and offended
Edwardian aesthetes and their followers – and
still does). The effect here is bold, brash and
vulgar, and the Cragside team is proud of it.

## The Italian Terrace

This is the centrepiece of the lowest level of the Formal Gardens. *The Loggia* stands against the middle of the revetment wall on the north. Built about 1870 (and restored in 1992–3), the building is typical of Armstrong's innovations, combining familiar forms and materials in a most individual way. It has a glass roof and sides, but an open front. The cast-iron sections were probably made at Armstrong's Elswick works.

Cast iron, the wonder material of the mid-Victorian age, was used for all the structural parts, including the columns, some of which also serve as downpipes. Each spring, tulips and hyacinths provide a riot of colour. The interior borders are planted with tender perennials every summer, giving a bright, exotic feeling. The oak seat, designed to incorporate the flat-topped 'A' which Armstrong used as a monogram elsewhere at Cragside, was made by Alan Forster in 2006 and funded by the Tynedale Association of the National Trust.

The raised stone borders to each side of the Loggia once had lean-to houses with detachable roofs. Since 1995 they have been planted with tender perennials, including species of Salvia and Penstemon from Mexico, Osteospermums

*(Below) The Loggia*

*The Cottage in the Park*

and Pelargoniums from South Africa, and other species also from warmer climes. Again, mass tulips brighten the spring.

## The Cottage in the Park

The house to the west of the Italian Terrace, once known as the Cottage in the Park, was built about 1865 for the estate manager, William Bertram, who lived here for over 40 years. The house has many features in common with the first part of Cragside itself and was presumably designed by the same unknown architect. It was extended to the west with an Estate Office about 1890. The building has now been converted into holiday cottages with spectacular views, and easy access to Rothbury.

## The Parkland

Lying to the south of the Formal Gardens, it is typical of the best undulating Northumberland pasture, sprinkled with clumps of beech and specimen ash and sycamore trees. Fine in itself, the parkland is also vital in views from the gardens across the Coquet valley.

### Restoring the Italian Terrace

Restoration of the central part of the Italian Terrace began in 2000 with the reinstatement of the quatrefoil pool. This had been removed in the 1920s to allow for tennis on the eastern part of the terrace. Luckily, the stonework had not travelled far and it was possible to reacquire it and give it pride of place once more at the centre of the terrace. On each side, wooden-framed enclosures (originally glazed) gave protection against wind. These were also removed in the 1920s, but have been restored (on the west in 2002, and the east in 2005, less the glazing, which would have been difficult to maintain). The enclosed borders have been replanted with plants with good foliage texture and scent, providing a contrast to the rest of the garden. The fine clematis collection mentioned in 1880 has been replanted. Many of the plants within the frameworks were considered to be half-hardy in Victorian times, such as Fuchsias, Nerines, Kniphofias and Calceolarias.

43

# Water for pleasure and power

His family used to joke that young Armstrong had water on the brain, but in fact he was so fascinated by its possibilities that the joke was little short of the plain truth. From his earliest days in Pandon Dene at Newcastle until the end of his life, he was at his most content when close to, or working with, water. He enjoyed it for its scenic beauty and for its recreational opportunities, but most of all he became absorbed by its potential power. The success of his early career was founded on the development of hydraulic lifting gear, and later when his business became principally known for its armaments, it was still hydraulic power which eased the heavy lifting involved in ironclad ship-building and in particular the handling of the great guns.

The choice of the site of Cragside was strongly influenced by the water courses and the topography, and its potential for creating hydraulic power. Debdon Burn and Black Burn could be dammed to create lakes, which added to the beauty of the landscape and provided opportunities for boating and angling; but the lakes, five in all, were also designed as reservoirs. Water could be distributed from them by a network of pipes for various uses across the estate. Most importantly, they provided a head of water which could be harnessed to drive a range of hydraulic machinery. Where possible, the water was put to successive uses.

The water from Debdon, the earliest of the lakes (and still part of the Armstrong estate to the west of the Alnwick Road) powered a turbine which operated the estate sawmill (and still does). This was also the site of the first experiments in producing hydro-electricity. Then the water ran into Tumbleton Lake, which was formed with a lower dam also

on the Debdon Burn. Here it became a head of water for the Pump House built below Tumbleton dam in 1866. Here pumps driven by a hydraulic engine provided water to the house. The pumps are a pair of opposite-displacement plunger pumps (essentially a linked pair of big water pistols: one powers the other, which squirts water to a reservoir above the house until an automatic switch reverses the roles). The apparatus, restored in 1986, can be seen working in the Pump House. Even then, the water has not finished its work, though it now becomes decorative. First, it falls over the series of water-falls in the Valley Garden below the house, passing beneath the Iron Bridge, and skirting the edge of the Pinetum before dropping dramatically through a gorge and running to meet the Coquet at Debdon Burnfoot.

To the east the Black Burn was similarly exploited. The main course of the burn was dammed to form the largest of the five lakes (though this was drained in the 1940s for safety reasons). The thatched boat house shows that the lake was used for boating, and possibly fishing, too. It was also a reservoir providing hydraulic power to a novel silage clamp at Cragend Farm, and maybe for other uses, too. Even more dramatic was the artificial feed

*(Right) Nelly's Moss Lake*

*(Above) Tumbleton Lake*

taken from the Black Burn high up on the moors. The water was carried first by a canal, which fed into a pipe, then in an open wooden flume, and finally along a stream to feed two new lakes on Nelly's Moss. The upper lake, which never seems to go dry, was equipped with a fishing hut. The lower lake provided a head of water for all the hydraulic machines at the house, and also was the source for the cascades in the Rock Gardens.

## Hydro-electric power

The final and most ambitious scheme, also derived from the Black Burn and Nelly's Moss, was to provide a 103m head of water to a turbine in the Power House built at Debdon Burnfoot in 1886. The turbine converted water pressure into circular motion to work a dynamo which generated electricity. The experiment was a success, with improved power supplies for lighting and other purposes both in the house and in other buildings on the estate. A second dynamo was added in 1895, using the same drive, but in this case charging batteries in the battery room which was added to the Power House. The only difficulty at some times was the lack of water. It seems that choices had to be made as to whether to have electric light or water in the cascades. To solve this problem, Armstrong installed a gas engine (he had funded the Rothbury gas works, too) to power the dynamos, when the turbine lacked water pressure. This meant a further extension to the Power House, which was used until 1945, when Cragside was connected to the mains supply from the National Grid.

Technological innovation was not confined to the house and immediate grounds; each of Armstrong's farms had its hydraulic pump to provide water or a turbine to drive agricultural machinery. As at the house, the innovations were intended to remove the drudgery of repetitive work and increase productivity.

# Caring for Cragside

## Looking after the house and landscape

When the National Trust first took on Cragside in 1977, there was much to understand and to restore, and there is still much to do now – but this is a reflection of the range and importance of the Armstrongs' original achievements.

The 'front line' staff who work at Cragside are supported by colleagues with regional or national responsibilities who offer expertise and consult the Trust's very wide circle of specialist advisers and contractors. Volunteers, who far outnumber the staff, provide help in many vital ways: for example, the house could not be opened without the help of volunteer room stewards and guides. Equally, the constant battle to keep miles of footpaths clear and safe is hugely assisted by those who regularly come on working holidays.

Maintenance work is carried out throughout the year on the house and collections, on other buildings, the gardens and the wider estate. Building inspections every five years are followed by programmes of works. Imagine as many as 100,000 guests arriving in your house each year, and you realise why there has to be daily cleaning. As far as the old house allows (it has over 180 spaces), the environment of the main rooms is controlled to help preserve more delicate items in the collection. In the winter 'putting-to-bed', there is more thorough cleaning, and all the contents are inspected and wrapped.

The conservation challenges extend far beyond the house. Historic machinery all around the estate has to be maintained in working order, although for conservation reasons some of it is not run very often. Trees have to be inspected, and drives, paths, bridges and steps maintained. And as attempts are made to achieve the Armstrongs' intended balance between woodland and open ground, more original features are discovered. In the gardens, as well as regular maintenance and seasonal planting, there is still much restoration to be done. Many operations involve archaeological investigation. Everywhere there is, too, the curatorial puzzle of how to combine

*(Right) The Prince of Wales's daughters exploring the Debdon Burn in 1884. Visitors have been welcome at Cragside from the start*

historical authenticity with effective and safe preservation. All has to be achieved with only a fraction of the workforce available to Lord Armstrong.

Those now responsible for Cragside recognise that it is a duty, as well as a privilege, to look after the place, to tell its story, and to give visitors an opportunity to understand its historical importance and to enjoy their time here. There is a duty, too, to balance our enjoyment against that of future generations. Through the application of careful conservation

*(Above) Maintaining the carpet bedding is a time-consuming task*

measures, we will pass on a property which is at least as interesting and enjoyable as that which we received.

All this conservation work, of course, is very expensive, and fund-raising is always an important part of the Trust's work. Much of this is done at Cragside itself. Those who enjoy their visit will tell their friends and will be more inclined to give help. This is why the work of those who staff the shop, restaurant and information centre, and those who maintain car-parks, lavatories and holiday cottages, is just as important as that of those more directly connected with care, conservation and security. All play their part, and so do you…..

## The future

Cragside has had so many major projects in recent years that one might imagine that most of the restoration is now complete. But this is not the case. In the immediate future it is hoped to restore the Iron Bridge and re-open it to visitors. Slightly further ahead will be the restoration of Lord Armstrong's Electrical Room in the house.

It is also hoped that before long it will be possible to reconnect the water supply to the Power House and to use a modern generator to provide hydro-electric heating and lighting in the building. More ambitiously, but ultimately essential to a full understanding of the gardens, will be the restoration of the great palm house with its smaller associated buildings, the ferneries, show house and orchid house.

There is also a continuing need to improve and develop methods of interpretation. No amount of excellent conservation work is much use unless visitors understand the significance of what is being done. The best interpretation must be interesting, informative and enjoyable. None of this will be worthwhile unless visitors' needs are also met. The usual catering and shopping facilities must be provided and maintained at a high standard. Our aim is to have happy, contented, well-fed visitors – amazed at Cragside – and keen to tell their friends! We *would* like to know how we can improve your visit.

Cragside is such an amazing place that it is very easy to forget how much it costs to maintain and restore. We are grateful for all financial help, without which restoration projects would not be possible. Miss Marjorie Lawson's generous legacy has funded the repair of the Orchard House, and the Cragside appeal has so far generated over 20,000 individual donations from people all over the country. Every one is appreciated.

### *Thank you*

By being a member, or paying to visit today, you, too, have supported our efforts to carry the wonders and spirit of Cragside safely into the future. Thank you very much. We hope you enjoy your visit, and that you will enjoy telling your friends about Cragside. We wish you a safe journey and hope you will return soon.